Seeds

by Grace Hansen

Abdo
PLANT ANATOMY
Kids

abdopublishing.com

Published by Abdo Kids, a division of ABDO, PO Box 398166, Minneapolis, Minnesota 55439.

Copyright © 2016 by Abdo Consulting Group, Inc. International copyrights reserved in all countries. No part of this book may be reproduced in any form without written permission from the publisher.

Printed in the United States of America, North Mankato, Minnesota.

102015

012016

Photo Credits: iStock, Science Source, Shutterstock

Production Contributors: Teddy Borth, Jennie Forsberg, Grace Hansen

Design Contributors: Laura Mitchell, Dorothy Toth

Library of Congress Control Number: 2015942107

Cataloging-in-Publication Data

Hansen, Grace.

 Seeds / Grace Hansen.

   p. cm. -- (Plant anatomy)

ISBN 978-1-68080-139-2 (lib. bdg.)

Includes index.

1. Seeds--Juvenile literature.   I. Title.

575.6/8--dc23

                    2015942107

Table of Contents

A Seed's Job

A seed has one job. It is to

make another plant of its kind.

Seed Parts

The outer layer is called the seed coat. It protects everything inside the seed.

seed coat

sunflower seed

seed coat

**chestnut
seed**

seed coat

**field
bean**

7

Inside each seed is a tiny plant. This plant is called an **embryo**. Embryos need water, oxygen, and warmth. Then they can grow!

embryo

9

Growing

When the **embryo** grows,

it breaks out of its seed.

This is called **germination**.

11

The **radicle** is the first thing

to grow from the seed.

The radicle is a young root.

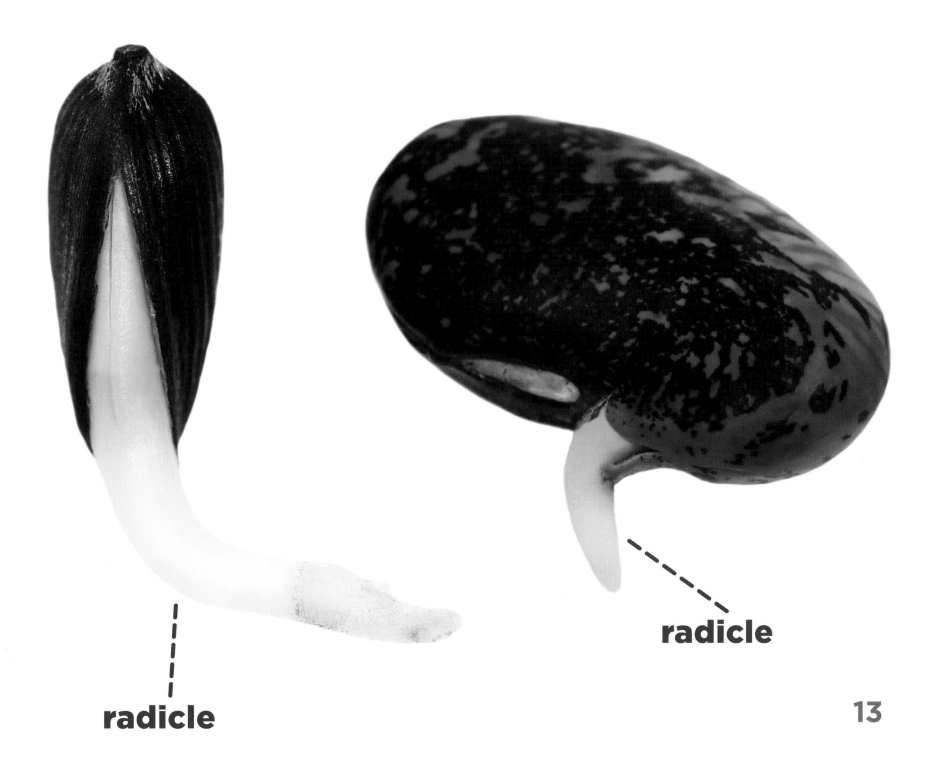

radicle

radicle

13

In some seeds, a young stem **emerges** next. It is called the **plumule**.

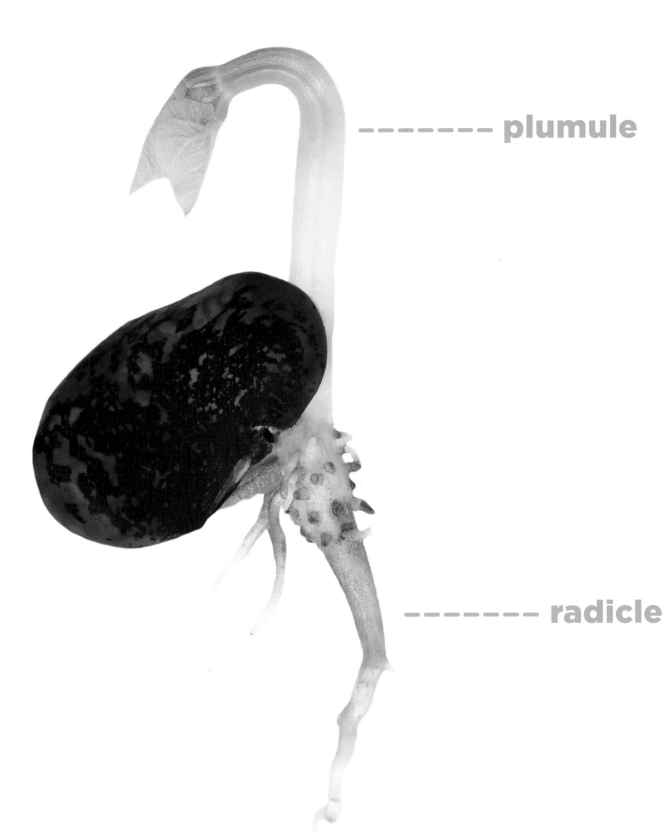

plumule

radicle

The stem and leaves grow toward the sun. Leaves use light to make food for the plant.

17

The roots grow downward. Roots collect water and food for the plant. The lower they grow, the more **nutrients** they find.

The plant is strong. Now a flower can grow. The flower's job is to make more seeds!

21

From Seed to Plant

Hypogeal

plumule

radicle

cotyledon

Epigeal

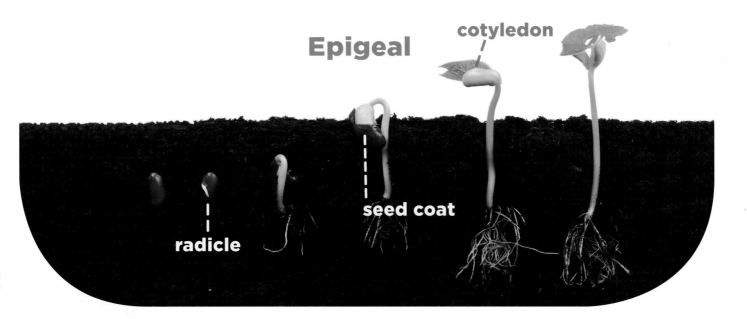

cotyledon

radicle

seed coat

22

Glossary

cotyledon – the first leaf of a seedling. It gives food to the plant until true leaves form.

embryo – the young, developing plant in the seed.

emerge – to come out of and into view.

epigeal – germination when the cotyledons emerge from underground and shed the seed coat.

germination – to begin to grow or develop into a plant.

hypogeal – germination when the cotyledons stay underground and inside the seed coat.

nutrient – something that gives nourishment for growth and health.

plumule – the young stem to grow from the seed of a plant. It will grow to become a stem and leaves.

radicle – the young root to emerge first from the seed.

23

Index

abdokids.com

Use this code to log on to abdokids.com and access crafts, games, videos, and more!

Abdo Kids Code:
PSK1392

DATE DUE

			PRINTED IN U.S.A.